A 31-DAY EXPERIMENT

Building a Strong
FAMILY

OTHER BOOKS BY DICK PURNELL

Building a Strong
FAMILY

DICK PURNELL

THOMAS NELSON PUBLISHERS
Nashville • Atlanta • London • Vancouver

Published in Nashville, Tennessee, by Thomas Nelson, Inc., Publishers, and distributed in Canada by Word Communications, Ltd., Richmond, British Columbia, and in the United Kingdom by Word (UK), Ltd., Milton Keynes, England.

Scripture quotations are taken from the HOLY BIBLE, NEW INTERNATIONAL VERSION ®. Copyright © 1973, 1978, 1984 by International Bible Society. Used by permission of Zondervan Bible Publishing House. All rights reserved.

The "NIV" and "New International Version" trademarks are registered in the United States Patent and Trademark Office by International Bible Society. Use of either trademark requires the permission of International Bible Society.

Library of Congress Cataloging-in-Publication Data

Purnell, Dick.
    Building a strong family / Dick Purnell.
        p.   cm. — (A 31-day experiment)
    ISBN 0-8407-6761-7 (pbk.)
    1. Christian education—Home training. 2. Family—Prayer-books and devotions—English. 3. Family—United States. 4. Devotional calendars. I. Title. II. Series: Purnell, Dick. 31-day experiment.
BV1590.P877 1994
248.8'45—dc20
                                                   93-3948
                                                     CIP

Printed in the United States of America
1 2 3 4 5 6 7 - 99 98 97 96 95 94

To My Family

Paula, Rachel and Ashley

*Together may we grow with God's help
to become a stronger family.*

CONTENTS

▼▼▼

WHAT GOD SAYS ABOUT RAISING CHILDREN

Wouldn't it be wonderful to sit down with the heavenly Father and ask Him what His guidelines and instructions are for building a strong home? If you're like me, you would probably listen with keen interest and take notes on everything He said.

Then you might say, "Lord, I have a question. What can I do to *apply* all You've told me about raising my children?"

That's the question I asked while I researched and wrote this book. I'm a parent of two girls, Rachel and Ashley, and the longing that has reverberated in me since they were born is this: *I want to be a good father.* I try hard. I work to understand my children better and develop the right attitudes and procedures to help them mature into fulfilled adults who enjoy life. Sometimes I think I am succeeding, other times I feel like a failure. Maybe you've felt the same way. Like me, do you ask: Who can tell me what to do—how to do this right?

We often look to someone else to help us become good parents. Many books offer opinions and suggestions by "experts." The thing is, these books may be good resources for families, but then again, human wisdom is limited. Who wants to risk a child's foundational well-being on solely human advice?

I believe that the clear answers and flawless guidelines we seek are readily provided for us by the Lord through His Word. That's the way I have structured this book. You will not find any of my opinions in these pages, nor advice from family specialists. This book is designed to help you glean parenting guidelines only from "the" expert: the heavenly Father Himself.

For the next 31 days you will have the privilege of privately conferring with the Master, discovering how you can become the best parent you can be. The book has two sections. The first, "Raising Your Children God's Way," will take you through sixteen biblical passages that reveal qualities that you as a parent should be developing. The second, "Life Principles to Teach Your Children," includes fifteen basic biblical teachings your children need to understand in order to live the way God intends.

It would be helpful for your spouse to do the Experiment at the same time. Pray for and with each other, and discuss what you are learning. Work together to do the projects with your children. It will be a great adventure for the whole family!

If you do not have a spouse or if your mate is unable to do the Experiment with you, ask a trusted Christian friend to pray for you as you work through the book. This will increase your confidence to trust God to teach you all you need to learn.

One last thought before you begin this Experiment: There are no perfect parents and there are no perfect children. Don't be afraid to fail. Try the daily projects, and trust God to give you success. Know that expressing desire and spending energy to be a godly parent are pleasing to the Lord, and He will help you.

A BIBLICAL PICTURE OF A FAMILY

Strong families and godly children are at the center of the biblical message. To give you an overview of what topics you will be studying for the next month, here are the titles for each of the 31 days.

SECTION 1 – RAISING YOUR CHILDREN GOD'S WAY:

1. The Ingredients of a Happy Family

2. Children: A Gift From God

3. Give Your Family to the Giver

4. Family Leadership Is Dad's Responsibility

5. Parenting As the Heavenly Father Does

6. A Generation Unlike Their Parents

7. Helping Your Children Know God

SECTION 2 – LIFE PRINCIPLES TO TEACH YOUR CHILDREN

MY PRAYER

Thank You, Lord, for giving me my wonderful children. Your goodness to me is overwhelming. What a privilege to have such a family.

Yet there are times that I forget Your generosity. Misunderstandings, arguments, anger, lack of communication, fear, discouragement, and a host of other negative things eat away at our family unity. We sometimes lose sight of Your instructions for building a strong family.

Heavenly Father, start with me. I admit to You that I have often sinned against You and my family. I am not a perfect parent.

Forgive my sins and change my life. Make me the kind of parent that You want me to be. Give me the qualities I need to build a family that pleases You. Teach me how to pass on a godly heritage to my children.

As I do this Experiment for the next 31 days, expand my understanding of Your Word and give me the strength to put Your instructions into practice.

I am relying on You, Lord, to show me the way to a stronger family. Unite my family in the bonds of love and understanding.

Signed_____

MY COVENANT
WITH GOD

I commit myself before God to do this Experiment in Building a Strong Family for the next 31 days. I make a covenant with the Heavenly Father to:

1. Spend 30 minutes or more each day in Bible study, prayer and writing out my thoughts and plans.

2. Ask my spouse or another Christian to pray daily for me that the Experiment will help me to become the kind of parent God wants me to be. (That person may want to do the Experiment along with you so you can share together what you are learning.)

3. Attend a church each week where the Word of God is taught.

Signed_____

Date _____

PROCESS TO DEVELOP A STRONG FAMILY

A. PREPARATION FOR EACH DAY

1. *Equipment:* Obtain a Bible to study and a pen to record your thoughts and plans in this book.
2. *Time:* Choose a specific half-hour each day to spend with the Lord. Pick the time of day that is best for you—when your heart is most responsive to meeting with God.
3. *Place:* Find a particular spot where you can clear your mind of distractions and focus your full attention on God's Word. Suggestions: bedroom, office, library, living room, lounge, outdoors.

B. READ—20 Minutes

1. Pray earnestly before you begin. Ask the Lord to teach you what He desires you to learn.
2. Read the entire passage.
3. Read it again, looking for important ideas.

4. Make written notes on the following:
   a. Sections A and B—study the passage thoroughly to answer the questions. Observe what God says about Himself and how you can live a dynamic, godly life. As you discover more of His truth, your understanding of God's purposes for you and your family will increase.
   b. Section C—Write out your personal responses to the Scripture you have studied. How, specifically, are you going to apply the lessons you learned to your life?
5. Choose a verse from the passage you have read that is especially meaningful to you. Copy it onto a card and read it several times during the day. Think about its meaning and impact on your life. Memorize it when you have free mental time, for example, when you are getting ready in the morning, while you are standing in line, taking a coffee break, relaxing in the evening, or walking somewhere.

C. NEED–5 Minutes
1. Pray that the Lord will give you insight into your family's needs.

2. Choose what is the most pressing need your family has for that day. It may be the same as on previous days or it may be a different one.
3. Write down your request. The more specific you are, the more specific the answer will be.
4. Earnestly pray for God's provision for that need. As you progress through the Experiment, exercise your developing faith. Trust God for big things.
5. When the Lord meets your need, record the date and how He did it. Periodically review God's wonderful provisions, and thank Him often for His faithfulness. This will greatly increase your faith and confidence in Him.
6. At the end of the month, review all the answers to your prayers. Rejoice in God's goodness to you. Keep praying for the requests that still need answers.

D. DEED–5 Minutes

1. Pray for God's guidance to do something for your family during that day. Try to apply the particular passage you have just studied.
2. Take the initiative to express in concrete ways God's wonderful love to your spouse and children. Be a servant. Someone has said, "Behind

every face there is a drama going on." Tap into their drama.

3. As you work on strengthening your family, determine to grow in your own relationship with Christ. Developing a strong faith in the Lord is the greatest goal in life.

4. Record the details of how the Holy Spirit used you this day. This will increase your confidence to trust God to develop other areas of your family. Make sure you don't allow pride to spoil the joy of giving. Thank the Lord Jesus for expressing His love and compassion through you.

E. PROJECT

1. Write down ideas about how you can put into practice specific lessons found in the passage.

2. Devise a plan to implement your ideas.

F. LAST THING IN THE EVENING

1. READ the passage again, looking for additional facts about God and about His ideas for strengthening your family.

2. Pray again for your NEED. Thank the Lord that He will answer in His way and in His time.

3. Record the DEED God guided you to accomplish.

4. Review the **PROJECT** you chose for the day.

G. PARTNERS

Ask your mate or another Christian to do the Experiment together with you. Pray frequently for one another that you will learn more about the Lord and how to develop a family built on His Word. Encourage one another to be disciplined and faithful in completing the Experiment. Set aside time each day to share what you are learning and pray together for God's power to unite your family together in His love. Help each other to apply what you are learning.

THE EXPERIMENT

31 Days

of

Building a
Strong Family

Section 1
Raising Your Children
God's Way
(Days 1-16)

THE INGREDIENTS OF A HAPPY FAMILY

Psalm 128:1–6

KEY VERSES:

Blessed are all who fear the LORD, who walk in his ways. You will eat the fruit of your labor; blessings and prosperity will be yours (Psalm 128:1–2).

TODAY'S FOCUS:

To fear the Lord means a person "stands in awe" of Him and honors Him. When a parent has an intimate relationship with God that is characterized by trust and obedience, it produces wonderful results in a family.

READ:

Pray to walk in God's ways.

A. When a person fears (reveres) the Lord, what will God do for that individual?

B. Even though life is filled with ups and downs, why do you think the Bible promises God's blessings for those who fear the Lord?

C. What changes do I need to make in my heart attitude toward the Lord?

DAY 1

NEED:

Pray to walk in His ways.

My family's greatest need today is:

God answered my prayers today _____ (date) in this way:

DEED:

Thank the Lord for His blessings on your family.

Lord, work in my family today by:

▲

PROJECT:

If you walked in God's ways more faithfully, how would that change your life and your relationship with your spouse and children? Make a list of those changes and ask the Lord to accomplish those things in your life and family.

CHILDREN: A GIFT FROM GOD

Psalm 127:1–5

KEY VERSES:

Sons are a heritage from the LORD, children a reward from him. Like arrows in the hands of a warrior are sons born in one's youth (Psalm 127:3–4).

TODAY'S FOCUS:

Your children are gifts from our wonderful Lord. Although they may bring both joy and heartache, your attitudes toward them will determine your relationship with them. Attitudes ultimately produce actions.

READ:

Pray for a thankful heart.

DAY 2

A. What attitude does God want you to have toward your children? Why?

B. How would you have felt if your parents had treated you as a heritage (gift) from God when you were young? How do you think your children would feel if you treated them as a gift from the Lord?

C. In what ways can I let the Lord be the builder of my home?

NEED:

Thank the Lord for giving you your children.

My family's greatest need today is:

God answered my prayers today _____ (date) in this way:

DEED:

Pray for your children.

O Lord, my attitude toward my children needs improving in the following areas:

▲

PROJECT:

God has given each of your children to you as a gift, on loan for a time. Write down the names of your children. Beside each name, indicate the positive aspects of that child's personality. Plan how you can communicate verbally your attitude of gratitude for them.

GIVE YOUR FAMILY
TO THE GIVER

Genesis 22:1–19

KEY VERSE:

"Do not lay a hand on the boy," he said. "Do not do anything to him. Now I know that you fear God, because you have not withheld from me your son, your only son" (Genesis 22:12).

TODAY'S FOCUS:

Our children are wonderful gifts from the Lord. Since He is the Giver, He wants us to commit them back to His ownership and guidance.

READ:

Pray to understand God's ownership of your children.

A. When Abraham was 100 years old, God gave him a son. When Isaac was probably a teenager, the Lord told Abraham to do something unusual. What was it? How did Abraham respond?

B. What did God do after Abraham obeyed Him?

C. In what ways do I need to give my children to the Lord for His ownership?

DAY 3

NEED:

Thank the Lord for providing for your family's needs.
My family's greatest need today is:

God answered my prayers today _____ (date) in this way:

DEED:

Pray for confidence to obey God in all areas of your life.
Dear God, the Bible contains Your commands to me.
Help me to:

▲

PROJECT:

Write out a prayer of commitment of your family to God.
Give Him total ownership of each person. Thank the
Lord that He is good and knows what is best for you and
your family at all times.

FAMILY LEADERSHIP IS DAD'S RESPONSIBILITY

1 Timothy 3:1–13

▼

KEY VERSE:

He must manage his own family well and see that his children obey him with proper respect (1 Timothy 3:4).

TODAY'S FOCUS:

Home leadership is a prerequisite, or training ground, for church leadership. How a man leads his family shows his qualifications to take on other significant leadership opportunities. Success in God's eyes starts with the home. Leaders are lovers.

READ:

Pray to manage your family well.

A. List and explain at least 10 characteristics of a godly leader.

B. Describe the impact your dad had on you, positive and/or negative. How could he have managed your family better?

C. To be a good family leader, I need to:

NEED:

Pray to be worthy of your children's respect.

My family's greatest need today is:

God answered my prayers today _____ (date) in this way:

DEED:

Pray that your children will obey you out of love and respect.

Heavenly Father, I want to be a person who lives in a manner that pleases You. Teach me to:

▲

PROJECT:

What areas of your life need to be brought into line with the list of characteristics of godly leaders found in this passage and in Titus 1:5–9? Choose one of those areas to endeavor to change today.

PARENTING AS THE HEAVENLY FATHER DOES

Psalm 103:1–22

KEY VERSES:
The LORD is compassionate and gracious, slow to anger, abounding in love.... As a father has compassion on his children, so the LORD has compassion on those who fear him; for he knows how we are formed, he remembers that we are dust (Psalm 103:8, 13–14).

TODAY'S FOCUS:
The greatest model of parenting that we have is our perfect heavenly Father. By examining the way He interacts with us, His children, we can learn how to parent our children more effectively.

READ:
Pray to be compassionate with your children.

DAY 5

A. How does the Lord relate to us?

B. How is God's compassion shown to us?

C. Because I want to imitate the Lord, I will:

NEED:

Praise God for His abounding love.

   My family's greatest need today is:

   God answered my prayers today _____ (date) in this way:

DEED:

Pray that you would reflect the parenting style of the Lord.

   Dear Lord, thank You for satisfying my desires with good things. Guide me to:

PROJECT:

How can you act more compassionately and graciously toward your children and spouse? Indicate some specific action points.

A GENERATION UNLIKE THEIR PARENTS

Judges 2:6–23

▼

KEY VERSES:

After that whole generation had been gathered to their fathers, another generation grew up, who knew neither the LORD nor what he had done for Israel. Then the Israelites did evil in the eyes of the LORD and served the Baals (Judges 2:10–11).

TODAY'S FOCUS:

Because a parent believes in and serves God does not mean that his or her children will automatically continue in that faith. God deals with each generation individually to bring them into a personal relationship with Him.

READ:

Pray for faithfulness to serve the Lord.

A. Joshua and his generation served the Lord faithfully. But what did their children do?

B. How did the Lord deal with that next generation?

C. Because I want to provide an atmosphere in my home that will encourage my children to want to walk with the Lord, I will:

DAY 6

NEED:

Thank the Lord that He wants every generation to know Him.

My family's greatest need today is:

God answered my prayers today _____ (date) in this way:

DEED:

Pray for God's understanding to know how to help your children serve the Lord.

O Lord, I need You to:

▲

PROJECT:

In what areas are your children showing signs of rebellion toward the Lord? Pray specifically for your children to become obedient to God in those areas. Ask yourself if you are doing anything to motivate them toward rebellion.

HELPING YOUR CHILDREN KNOW GOD

Psalm 78:1–22

KEY VERSES:

He decreed statutes for Jacob and established the law in
Israel, which he commanded our forefathers to teach their
children, so the next generation would know them, even
the children yet to be born, and they in turn would tell
their children (Psalm 78:5–6).

TODAY'S FOCUS:

If the knowledge of God is to continue to spread, we must
teach the next generation about who He really is and what
He has done. We must also live what we tell them. By our
lips and lives we communicate what it means to walk with
God.

READ:

Pray for wisdom to teach your children about the Lord.

DAY 7

A. Why does God want you to teach your children about Him? How does He want you to do this?

B. What did their forefathers and the men of Ephraim (and of all Israel) do that your children should avoid?

C. Because I want my life to be consistent with what I teach my children about the Lord, I will:

NEED:

Praise the Lord for His deeds, power, and the wonders He has performed.

My family's greatest need today is:

God answered my prayers today _____ (date) in this way:

DEED:

Pray for your children to genuinely trust God with their lives.

Dear Lord, help me to tell my children about:

▲

PROJECT:

The Hebrew teaching style was for parents to take their children with them and teach them about God by showing, explaining, asking questions, listening, etc. How will you go about communicating biblical truths to your children? Concentrate on one area today where you can demonstrate to your children and instruct them how to trust in God.

PASS ON LIVING TRUTH

2 Timothy 1:1–14

▼

KEY VERSES:

I have been reminded of your sincere faith, which first lived in your grandmother Lois and in your mother Eunice and, I am persuaded, now lives in you also. For this reason I remind you to fan into flame the gift of God, which is in you through the laying on of my hands (2 Timothy 1:5–6).

TODAY'S FOCUS:

Faith in Jesus Christ is an individual matter that a person must decide on for him- or herself. But transferring to the next generation truth that you have lived is a wonderful legacy that will encourage your children to follow Christ also.

READ:

Pray that your children will have a sincere faith.

A. Timothy was Paul's spiritual son through his ministry. What had Timothy received from the people who loved him?

B. What does Paul encourage Timothy to do?

C. I want to help my children discover and develop their unique gifts by:

DAY 8

NEED:

Praise the Lord for His grace.

My family's greatest need today is:

God answered my prayers today _____ (date) in this way:

DEED:

Pray for your children to guard the "good deposit," which is the gospel.

Dear Lord Jesus, thank You that You have brought life and immortality to me. Help me to bring that same message to my loved ones by:

▲

PROJECT:

Choose a specific time and place when you and your spouse will lay your hands on each of your children in a special family ceremony. Dedicate them to the Lord, and ask Him to motivate each one to utilize their God-given gifts to the greatest extent possible.

REMEMBER THE SIGNIFICANT EVENTS

Joshua 4:1–24

KEY VERSES:

He said to the Israelites, "In the future when your descendants ask their fathers, 'What do these stones mean?' tell them, 'Israel crossed the Jordan on dry ground. For the LORD your God dried up the Jordan before you until you had crossed over'" (Joshua 4:21–23).

TODAY'S FOCUS:

We so quickly forget—especially the good things God does for us. Helping your family to remember will increase their confidence in the Lord.

READ:

Pray to remember significant events in your life when God taught you important lessons.

A. What command did God give the people of Joshua's
    time that would influence their descendants?

B. Give the purpose of the twelve stones.

C. Here is a memorial I will establish so that my family
    and I will remember an important lesson God taught
    us:

NEED:

Pray for God's power.

My family's greatest need today is:

God answered my prayers today _____ (date) in this way:

DEED:

Pray for your family to fear the Lord.

O Lord God, direct me to:

▲

PROJECT:

Think back on your family history. What specific things has God done for you that you want your children to remember always? Design a memorial to the Lord and tell your children about its significance.

GIVE YOUR DREAMS AWAY

1 Chronicles 28:1–21

▼

KEY VERSES:

My son Solomon, acknowledge the God of your father, and serve him with wholehearted devotion and with a willing mind, for the LORD searches every heart and understands every motive behind the thoughts. If you seek him, he will be found by you; but if you forsake him, he will reject you forever. Consider now, for the LORD has chosen you to build a temple as a sanctuary. Be strong and do the work (1 Chronicles 28:9–10).

TODAY'S FOCUS:

When God gives you a personal dream, He may want to fulfill it through your children. We should not attempt to live our lives through our children, nor force our goals on them. However, we can share our personal dreams and help our children see that God has a unique purpose for their lives.

READ:

Pray to be a godly vision-builder in your family.

DAY 10

A. David had a goal to build the temple of the Lord. But God said that David's son Solomon would be the builder. In his love for God and Solomon, David transferred his plans and vision to his son. What did David do to help Solomon accomplish the task?

B. How did David encourage his son to trust God?

C. I believe that God has a special plan for each of my children. Here is how I will endeavor to help them realize that:

DAY 10

NEED:

Thank the Lord that He is with you and your children.

My family's greatest need today is:

God answered my prayers today _____ (date) in this way:

DEED:

Pray that your children will be wholeheartedly devoted to the Lord.

Wonderful Lord, thank You for giving me all I possess. Open my heart toward my children to:

▲

PROJECT:

How can you instill vision and godly purpose into your children? Without trying to live your life through them, think of ways you can motivate your children to trust God to accomplish His purposes for their lives. How can you help them achieve great things for the Lord?

GIVE YOUR RESOURCES AWAY

1 Chronicles 29:1–25

▼

KEY VERSES:

Then King David said to the whole assembly: "My son Solomon, the one whom God has chosen, is young and inexperienced. The task is great, because this palatial structure is not for man but for the LORD God. With all my resources I have provided for the temple of my God" (1 Chronicles 29:1–2).

TODAY'S FOCUS:

Your children are unique creations made by God to fulfill a special part of His magnificent plan. As parents we need to use our resources to help our children fulfill God's will for them in His way and in His time.

READ:

Pray for joyful generosity toward your children.

A. David assembled all the leaders and key people in the nation. How did he motivate them to help Solomon accomplish the task of building the temple of God?

B. How did he acknowledge that the Lord was the director of the project and not himself?

C. I am trusting the Lord to:

DAY 11

NEED:

Praise the Lord that He is head over all.

My family's greatest need today is:

God answered my prayers today _____ (date) in this way:

DEED:

Pray for wisdom to motivate others to serve God.

O Lord, God of Israel, everything I have comes from You. Because You own my resources, show me:

▲

PROJECT:

What resources do you have in the following areas: faith in the Lord, spiritual gifts, positive attitudes, character qualities, possessions? List them and ask God to guide you in giving them to your children.

ENCOURAGE INDEPENDENCE

Luke 2:21–51

▼

KEY VERSE:

The child grew and became strong; he was filled with wisdom, and the grace of God was upon him (Luke 2:40).

TODAY'S FOCUS:

Dedicating your children to the Lord means that they are under His leadership. He may guide them differently than you expect. They need to develop their own personal faith in Him.

READ:

Pray for your children to follow God's leadership.

A. Mary and Joseph went to the temple to present Jesus
to the Lord. What happened that further confirmed
to them that God had special plans for their child?

B. When Jesus was twelve years old, what did His
parents learn that furthered their understanding of
what God was doing in their son's life?

C. I want my children to have their own faith in God
because:

NEED:

Thank God for giving us Jesus.

My family's greatest need today is:

God answered my prayers today _____ (date) in this way:

DEED:

Pray to trust God's dealing with your children.

Sovereign Lord, I commit my children to You and ask that:

▲

PROJECT:

As an earthly parent your responsibilities are to provide for your children and pass on to them what God has taught you. But have you ever released your children to God's care? List the things that hinder you from entrusting them totally to Him. Beside each obstacle indicate how you will overcome that hindrance. Place your children in His hands. Get ready for surprises!

DISCIPLINE YOUR CHILDREN PROPERLY

Proverbs 23:12–35

▼

KEY VERSES:
Do not withhold discipline from a child; if you punish him with the rod, he will not die. Punish him with the rod and save his soul from death (Proverbs 23:13–14).

TODAY'S FOCUS:
Disciplining a child is not easy for the child—or the parent. But correction with love produces character qualities that will eventually bring joy to both parent and child.

READ:
Pray for wisdom to properly discipline your children.

DAY 13

A. What are the purposes of discipline?

B. Read Proverbs 13:24; 19:18; 22:6, 15; 29:15, 17. In
    addition, study Ephesians 6:4 and Colossians 3:21.
    What are proper motives to have when you discipline
    your children?

C. Because I desire to discipline my children with the
    proper motives, I will:

NEED:

Pray that your relationship with your children will improve.

My family's greatest need today is:

God answered my prayers today _____ (date) in this way:

DEED:

Pray to discipline your children in love, not in anger.

O Lord, teach me to:

▲

PROJECT:

Describe an incident when you were disciplined by your parents. What impact did it have on you? How does this help you in disciplining your children now? How do today's passages affect the way you will discipline your children in the future?

CHILDREN NEED BOUNDARIES

1 Samuel 2:12–17, 22–36

KEY VERSE:
Why do you honor your sons more than me? (1 Samuel 2:29).

TODAY'S FOCUS:
The guidelines for raising children are found in God's Word. The Lord wants us to be students of our children and train them according to God's ways. If you leave children to govern themselves, they will follow their sinful natures. Providing boundaries helps children know how they should behave. As a result they will feel secure and loved.

READ:
Pray for an honest look at the way you are raising your children.

A. Eli was the high priest of Israel. Although he was a godly man, he was a weak father. Why was God angry with him?

B. Read 1 Samuel 4:1–22. How did God punish Eli and his wicked sons?

C. Because I want to be a consistently effective parent, I will:

DAY 14

NEED:
Pray that God will establish your home.
My family's greatest need today is:

God answered my prayers today _____ (date) in this way:

DEED:
Pray for courage to guide your children.
Lord, I need Your strength to:

———▲———

PROJECT:
List some wrong attitudes and actions that your children need to correct. What boundaries can you set to help them change? How will you express your love and care for them at the same time you are giving and maintaining those boundaries?

GO TO THE RIGHT PLACE FOR ANSWERS

Mark 9:14–29

▼

KEY VERSES:
"Teacher, I brought you my son, who is possessed by a spirit that has robbed him of speech. . . . I asked your disciples to drive out the spirit, but they could not" (Mark 9:17–18).

TODAY'S FOCUS:
No matter how easy it is to talk with your friends and Christian leaders about a problem, ultimately it is the Lord Jesus who is the source of healing. In His time and in His way He will provide the answer.

READ:
Pray that your faith will increase.

A. How did the father try to help his son?

B. What did Jesus say was the way to find an answer for problems?

C. Since Christ is the source for healing, I will go to Him for:

NEED:

Pray that the Lord will help you overcome unbelief.

My family's greatest need today is:

God answered my prayers today _____ (date) in this way:

DEED:

Pray that you will have an opportunity to help someone outside your family today.

Dear Lord Jesus, I believe that You will:

PROJECT:

What difficult problems is your family facing? Develop a prayer request list of those things and come to Christ each day, trusting Him for His solutions.

UNITE ALL GENERATIONS TOGETHER IN LOVE

Ruth 4:1–21

▼

KEY VERSES:

So Boaz took Ruth and she became his wife. And the LORD enabled her to conceive, and she gave birth to a son. The women said to Naomi: "Praise be to the LORD, who this day has not left you without a kinsman-redeemer. May he become famous throughout Israel!" (Ruth 4:13–14)

TODAY'S FOCUS:

God wants extended families (parents, children, grandparents, and relatives) to be united in love and respect. Having strong family bonds brings joy.

READ:

Pray for unity with your parents and relatives.

A. All that Naomi had left after her husband and two sons died was her daughter-in-law, Ruth. Through some unusual circumstances, God brought Ruth into contact with Boaz, who became her kinsman-redeemer. According to Israel's law, it was the duty of the closest male relative to redeem the deceased person's property and his widow. Even though Boaz was not Ruth and Naomi's closest relative, how did he redeem them?

B. How did the Lord use Boaz to bless Naomi?

C. This is what I would like to do for my parents and relatives:

NEED:

Thank the Lord that He cares for all generations.
   My family's greatest need today is:

   God answered my prayers today _____ (date) in this
   way:

DEED:

Pray for a united family.
   Dear Lord, use me to unite all generations of my family
   by:

▲

PROJECT:

Write out the names of your close relatives and in-laws.
In what ways would you like the Lord to use you to bring
greater harmony and communication among family
members? Be specific. Pray about it and take steps to put
your ideas into action.

THE EXPERIMENT

31 Days

of

Building a Strong Family

Section 2
Life Principles
to Teach Your Children
(Days 17-31)

LOVE GOD ABOVE ALL ELSE

Deuteronomy 6:1–25

KEY VERSES:
Love the LORD your God with all your heart and with all your soul and with all your strength. These commandments that I give you today are to be upon your hearts. Impress them on your children. Talk about them when you sit at home and when you walk along the road, when you lie down and when you get up (Deuteronomy 6:5–7).

TODAY'S FOCUS:
As Israel was getting ready to enter the Promised Land, Moses instructed the people how to build a great nation and godly families. He said that loving God is the greatest purpose in life.

READ:
Pray for a greater love for the Lord.

DAY 17

A. What can you do to help your children love God?

B. Your children know what you love the most by watching your life. How, then, could you better love God and demonstrate your commitment to Him?

C. I love the Lord God because:

NEED:

Pray for your children to love God.

My family's greatest need today is:

God answered my prayers today _____ (date) in this way:

DEED:

Pray for wisdom to instruct your children.

O Lord God, give me an opportunity today to teach my children about:

▲

PROJECT:

Choose one thing about the Lord you love. Write down ideas about how you will teach that to your children.

FULFILLMENT COMES FROM A RELATIONSHIP WITH GOD

Psalm 112:1–10

▼

KEY VERSES:

Blessed is the man who fears the LORD, who finds great delight in his commands. His children will be mighty in the land; the generation of the upright will be blessed (Psalm 112:1–2).

TODAY'S FOCUS:

To "fear the Lord" means to have reverential awe toward God. It is a humble attitude and trust that come from understanding the greatness of the Lord. Your relationship with Him will have a profound effect on your family.

READ:

Pray for a more intimate relationship with the Lord.

DAY 18

A. How is a family affected when a parent fears the Lord?

B. What else does God do for a person who is awed by His greatness?

C. Because I want to "fear" the Lord even more, I will:

NEED:

Praise the Lord for all He has done for you.

My family's greatest need today is:

God answered my prayers today _____ (date) in this way:

DEED:

Pray that your children will fear the Lord.

O wonderful Lord, how thankful I am for Your goodness to my family. Give me the power to:

▲

PROJECT:

List all the attributes of God that you're aware of. Find verses that explain these qualities. Because He is an awesome God, praise Him for who He is and what He has done. Think of what you can do to help your children to establish a life-long reverence for the Lord.

THE GREATEST LIFE
STARTS WITH THE LORD

Proverbs 1:1–33

KEY VERSE:
The fear of the LORD is the beginning of knowledge, but
fools despise wisdom and discipline (Proverbs 1:7).

TODAY'S FOCUS:
God said to Solomon, the writer of Proverbs, "Wisdom
and knowledge will be given you" (2 Chronicles 1:12). As
a wise father, Solomon instructed his son how to live.
Following Solomon's advice, parents should live wisely,
not foolishly, and instruct their children to do the same.

READ:
Pray for your children to listen to God's Word.

A. Wisdom begins with the understanding that the Lord knows best how we should live. What reasons did Solomon give for writing the Proverbs to his son?

B. What will happen if your children reject God's wisdom?

C. I want my children to be wise because:

DAY 19

NEED:

Pray that your children will acquire a disciplined and prudent life.

My family's greatest need today is:

God answered my prayers today _____ (date) in this way:

DEED:

Pray for the ability to instill wisdom in your children.

Lord, help me to:

▲

PROJECT:

Think of creative ways to encourage your children to think biblically (wisely). Things on TV, events at school, and statements made by their friends provide opportunities for you to help them ask the question: "What would a wise person do in this situation?"

SEEK WISDOM BEFORE YOU SEEK WEALTH

Proverbs 2:1–22

KEY VERSES:

For the LORD gives wisdom, and from his mouth come knowledge and understanding. He holds victory in store for the upright, he is a shield to those whose walk is blameless, for he guards the course of the just and protects the way of his faithful ones (Proverbs 2:6–8).

TODAY'S FOCUS:

Motivating children to walk on the right path of life is a challenge. But God can give the knowledge and insight needed for a parent to do the job.

READ:

Pray for your children to gain wisdom.

A. If your children pursue biblical wisdom and discernment, how will they be affected?

B. Discernment delivers us from what?

C. To motivate my children to be wise, I must be wise myself. Here is how I will pursue wisdom:

NEED:

Pray for patience.

My family's greatest need today is:

God answered my prayers today _____ (date) in this way:

DEED:

Pray for opportunities to teach wisdom.

O Lord, as a parent I need wisdom to:

▲

PROJECT:

Peer pressure is a very strong influence on your children. Think of creative ways to encourage them to choose godly friends rather than ungodly ones. Teach them to discern between wisdom and wickedness.

HUMAN UNDERSTANDING IS LIMITED

Proverbs 3:1–35

KEY VERSES:

Trust in the LORD with all your heart and lean not on your own understanding; in all your ways acknowledge him, and he will make your paths straight (Proverbs 3:5–6).

TODAY'S FOCUS:

God's wisdom is better than the riches of the world. Helping your children trust Him will set them on the right path of life.

READ:

Pray for a deeper trust in God.

DAY 21

A. Solomon admonished his son to remember his teaching. What important things should children do?

B. How would children benefit from doing those things?

C. In what specific ways can I model trusting in the Lord with all my heart?

NEED:

Pray for your children to turn away from evil.

My family's greatest need today is:

God answered my prayers today _____ (date) in this way:

DEED:

Pray for your children to acknowledge the Lord in all their ways.

Lord, I want You to help me be a model of acknowledging You in all my ways. Here is an area of my life in which I need Your wisdom today:

▲

PROJECT:

Think of a way to help your children grow in their confidence to trust the Lord. Ask God to give you opportunities to show them that human understanding is limited, but God's understanding is always right.

THE BEST LIFE GOES TO THE RIGHTEOUS

Proverbs 4:1–27

▼

KEY VERSE:

The path of the righteous is like the first gleam of dawn, shining ever brighter till the full light of day (Proverbs 4:18).

TODAY'S FOCUS:

Children are tempted in many ways to do wrong. When they seek to live righteously, they will always be thankful.

READ:

Pray for a righteous life.

A. Solomon received good advice from his father David. What was it?

B. What are the benefits of living the way God wants us to live?

C. I desire to live a wise and righteous life because:

DAY 22

NEED:

Pray for your children to guard their hearts.
  My family's greatest need today is:

  God answered my prayers today _____ (date) in this
  way:

DEED:

Pray for your children to avoid wickedness.
  Heavenly Father, I pray that my children will:

▲

PROJECT:

Write down some wise advice you received from your
parents or some other significant person during your
childhood. Share that advice with your children. How
did it help you live a better life?

SEX WITHIN MARRIAGE IS BEAUTIFUL

Proverbs 5:1–23

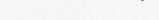

KEY VERSES:

May your fountain be blessed, and may you rejoice in the wife of your youth. A loving doe, a graceful deer—may her breasts satisfy you always, may you ever be captivated by her love (Proverbs 5:18–19).

TODAY'S FOCUS:

God has designed sex for marriage and only marriage. He is the creator of men and women and the architect of marriage. Following His Word will lead to the kind of joyful intimate relationship He intended.

READ:

Pray for your children to remain sexually pure until marriage.

A. Why should a person stay away from adultery?

B. What are the benefits of sex within a loving marriage?

C. I believe sexual intercourse is reserved by God only
    for a marriage relationship because:

DAY 23

NEED:

Thank God that He watches all paths of your family.
My family's greatest need today is:

God answered my prayers today _____ (date) in this
way:

DEED:

Pray for your children to listen to godly instruction.
Dear God, show me how to instruct my children to:

▲

PROJECT:

Talk with each of your children privately about sex and
God's design for an intimate marriage relationship. List
all the positive reasons for reserving sexual intercourse
until marriage. Give them a good picture of what God
intends for marriage to be like.

SEX OUTSIDE MARRIAGE IS DESTRUCTIVE

Proverbs 6:16–35

▼

KEY VERSES:

Do not lust in your heart after her beauty or let her captivate you with her eyes, for the prostitute reduces you to a loaf of bread, and the adulteress preys upon your very life (Proverbs 6:25–26).

TODAY'S FOCUS:

Our culture bombards us with sexual temptations. Your children need parents who strongly hold onto biblical values. They need you to help them be victorious over sexual temptation.

READ:

Pray that your children will overcome sexual temptation.

A.   What does the Lord hate?

B.   How does immorality affect a person?

C.   Have you been sexually pure in your thoughts and
     actions? What has this passage motivated you to do
     in your own life?

NEED:

Pray that your children will listen to God's Word.

My family's greatest need today is:

God answered my prayers today _____ (date) in this way:

DEED:

Pray that your children will develop inner convictions about remaining sexually pure.

Lord, help me to guide my children to:

▲

PROJECT:

Many children who get involved sexually before marriage are actually starved for non-sexual physical and emotional affection. In what ways can you strengthen your relationship with your children to help them defend against the sexual pressures they will inevitably face?

(Note: If they have already become involved, they need forgiveness and practical steps for restoration to purity. My book *Free to Love Again: Coming to Terms With Sexual Regret* offers practical advice for helping people with this important issue.)

SAY "NO!"
TO SEXUAL PRESSURE

Proverbs 7:1–27

KEY VERSE:

Do not let your heart turn to her ways or stray into her paths (Proverbs 7:25).

TODAY'S FOCUS:

Giving in to sexual temptation has disastrous results. Your children need to be warned of the consequences of immorality. They also need your example of moral purity and your heartfelt understanding of their sexuality.

READ:

Pray for God's grace.

A.   Describe the temptations the young man faced.

B.   Describe the results of his immoral behavior.

C.   Because I desire to help my children in this area, I will:

DAY 25

NEED:

Pray that your children will have the strength and wisdom to overcome sexual temptation.

My greatest need today is:

God answered my prayers today _____ (date) in this way:

DEED:

Pray your children will want to listen to God's instructions.

Lord, my children need to know:

▲

PROJECT:

How will you teach your children to say "No!" to sexual pressure? Ask them what kind of sexual temptations they are facing. Design a specific plan that will strengthen their resolve in overcoming these sexual enticements. Help them think of ways to handle their sexual desires in a biblical and satisfying manner. Remember the saying, "He who fails to plan, plans to fail."

LIVE BY THE TEN COMMANDMENTS

Exodus 20:1–20

KEY VERSE:

Honor your father and your mother, so that you may live long in the land the LORD your God is giving you (Exodus 20:12).

TODAY'S FOCUS:

God gave the "Ten Commandments." They are not the "Ten Suggestions." He wants all people to obey them. Therefore, it is crucial that your children know and abide by these direct commands.

READ:

Pray for a responsive heart.

DAY 26

A. Before the Israelites entered the Promised Land, the Lord gave them commands by which to live and to raise their families. List and explain each of the commands.

1.

2.

3.

4.

5.

6.

7.

8.

9.

10.

B. Why did God give the Ten Commandments?

C. I want my children to live by these commands because:

NEED:

Pray for God's power to obey them yourself.

My family's greatest need today is:

God answered my prayers today _____ (date) in this way:

DEED:

Pray for forgiveness when you break one.

O Lord, You are awesome! Help me to reverence You much more deeply so that:

▲

PROJECT:

How are you doing in obeying the Ten Commandments? James says, "Whoever keeps the whole law and yet stumbles at just one point is guilty of breaking all of it" (James 2:10). If you are involved in breaking any of these commands, confess your sins to God and accept His forgiveness. Turn from your sinful ways and obey God's laws. Write down ideas as to how you will teach your children to do the same thing.

YOU ARE FULLY KNOWN AND FULLY UNDERSTOOD

Psalm 139:1–24

▼

KEY VERSES:

For you created my inmost being; you knit me together in my mother's womb. I praise you because I am fearfully and wonderfully made; your works are wonderful, I know that full well (Psalm 139:13–14).

TODAY'S FOCUS:

Our knowledge of ourselves and our family is limited. When children realize that God knows them totally, understands them completely, and loves them unconditionally, they feel secure in a personal relationship with Him.

READ:

Pray for insight.

A. What does God know about you and each member of your family?

B. Why can you entrust yourself and each member of your family to the Lord?

C. I want to help my children understand that God knows them totally and has their best interests in His heart. Here are some ideas how I will try to do this:

NEED:

Praise God that He is the Creator.

My family's greatest need today is:

God answered my prayers today _____ (date) in this way:

DEED:

Give thanks for the Holy Spirit's presence.

O God, I place each person in my family into Your hands. You know that:

▲

PROJECT:

Write down the names of your family members. What about each one makes you fearful? How does understanding God's knowledge of them and His presence with them help you overcome anxiety?

PROPER DISCIPLINE IS GOOD FOR YOU

Hebrews 12:1–12

▼

KEY VERSE:

No discipline seems pleasant at the time, but painful. Later on, however, it produces a harvest of righteousness and peace for those who have been trained by it (Hebrews 12:11).

TODAY'S FOCUS:

God disciplines us because we are His children. His motives and purposes are the model for how we should discipline our children and how children should understand parental correction.

READ:

Pray for a teachable attitude.

A. Why does God discipline us?

B. What does loving discipline produce in a child?

C. My motives in disciplining my children are:

DAY 28

NEED:

Thank God that He loves you and your children.

My family's greatest need today is:

God answered my prayers today _____ (date) in this way:

DEED:

Pray that your children will respond properly to loving discipline.

My wonderful God, give me wisdom to:

▲

PROJECT:

Read these Proverbs—3:11–12; 6:23–24; 12:1; 13:1, 18; 15:5, 10, 32; 19:20, 27. Think of ways you can help your children accept loving discipline with a godly attitude.

REPENTANCE AND FORGIVENESS GO TOGETHER

Luke 15:11–32

▼

KEY VERSE:
For this son of mine was dead and is alive again; he was lost and is found (Luke 15:24).

TODAY'S FOCUS:
Forgiveness is difficult when a child has deeply disappointed or offended a parent. But repenting opens the door for a child to receive Mom and Dad's forgiveness, thereby making reconciliation possible.

READ:
Pray for courage to forgive your children.

A. Describe what the boy did.

B. How did the father respond to the boy's return?

C. Because I want reconciliation and healing in my relationship with my children, I will:

DAY 29

NEED:

Pray that your children will humbly repent when they
have sinned.

My family's greatest need today is:

God answered my prayers today _____ (date) in this
way:

DEED:

Pray for compassion.

Dear Savior, You forgave me all my sins. When I think
of my children's sins, fill me with Your compassion to:

▲

PROJECT:

What have your children done that has hurt you? Have
you genuinely forgiven them? How will you endeavor to
bring reconciliation?

THE WAY TO THE TOP
STARTS AT THE BOTTOM

Matthew 20:17–28

▼

KEY VERSES:

Whoever wants to become great among you must be your servant, and whoever wants to be first must be your slave (Matthew 20:26–27).

TODAY'S FOCUS:

Our natural tendency is to seek to become the leader and have power over people. But Christ's perspective directs us to serve others—even when we become the leader.

READ:

Pray that you would model for your children what it means to serve others.

A. The mother of James and John (Zebedee's sons) wanted her children to be leaders and get the glory. How did Jesus react to her motherly request?

B. How did Jesus show He lived by His own advice?

C. I desire to live by what Jesus taught and demonstrated. Therefore, I will:

NEED:

Thank Christ He came to earth as a servant-leader.
    My family's greatest need today is:

    God answered my prayers today _____ (date) in this way:

DEED:

Pray your children will become servant-leaders.
    Dear Lord Jesus, teach me to:

▲

PROJECT:

What qualities would a servant-leader need to possess? Do you practice these qualities yourself? Choose the three most important ones and teach them to your children this week. Seek specific ways to serve your family today.

MAKE YOUR WALK
MATCH YOUR TALK

1 John 2:1–17

▼

KEY VERSES:
If anyone obeys his word, God's love is truly made
complete in him. This is how we know we are in him:
Whoever claims to live in him must walk as Jesus did
(1 John 2:5–6).

TODAY'S FOCUS:
The person who follows God's Word will see a greater
love between family members and a life reflective of the
Lord's life. The values of the world are opposite the
values of a person who walks as Jesus did. The great
challenge is to live our biblical convictions day in and day
out.

READ:
Thank Christ, the Righteous One, that your sins are
forgiven.

A. What does "knowing" God involve, and how does it affect our everyday lives?

B. If you know God, how will that affect the way you treat your family members?

C. Does your walk match your talk? In what areas do you need to recommit yourself to doing the will of God?

NEED:

Pray to overcome the evil one.

My family's greatest need today is:

God answered my prayers today _____ (date) in this way:

DEED:

Pray that your children will walk as Jesus did.

Father, I want to know You more deeply and to:

▲

PROJECT:

Rewrite verses 15–17 in your own words. How can you teach them to your children? How can you guide them to walk as Jesus did and to live authentic Christian lives?

ACTION POINTS

Well, how did you do?

After a month of spending time with God and His Word, your heart is probably filled with thanksgiving for all He has taught you. It has been hard work, but well worth the effort.

During this time you have learned many things that will help you deepen your relationship with your children and guide them to live a life pleasing to God. It is possible to get overloaded with information and fail to apply what you have learned. This section is designed to help you condense all of the information you have received while working through this book.

Review all the truths you have learned and the projects you have done for the last 31 days. Which ones are the most vital for you to continue to work on? Select the top three action points you want to focus on for the next six months. If you accomplish these three, you will make significant progress in strengthening your family.

ACTION POINT #1 – _____

_____

_____

_____

ACTION POINT #2 – _____

_____

_____

_____

ACTION POINT #3 – _____

_____

_____

_____

Continue to work on these projects until you have completed them to your satisfaction. Pick new projects and goals to accomplish. At least once a year analyze each of your children and devise goals and projects to help them to become what God wants them to be.

RESOURCES FOR YOUR FAMILY: PRACTICAL ADVICE FROM PSALMS AND PROVERBS

Scattered throughout the Psalms and Proverbs are beautiful gems of God's wisdom concerning family matters. He is the heavenly Father who knows how to parent children and to instruct them in His ways so they will have wisdom to develop their lives.

Here are His statements to guide you in building a strong family. There are two sections. The first is directed toward you to guide you in shaping your thoughts and behavior. With the privileges and responsibilities you have as a parent you need God's wisdom.

The second section focuses on God's wisdom for your children to know and apply. Their future happiness depends on their internalizing these biblical principles and incorporating them into their lives.

A. Advice for Parents

YOUR BEHAVIOR AFFECTS YOUR CHILDREN

Proverbs 24:3
By wisdom a house is built, and through understanding it is established.

Proverbs 15:6
The house of the righteous contains great treasure, but the income of the wicked brings them trouble.

Psalm 37:28
For the LORD loves the just and will not forsake his faithful ones. They will be protected forever, but the offspring of the wicked will be cut off.

Proverbs 14:1
The wise woman builds her house, but with her own hands the foolish one tears hers down.

Proverbs 17:1
Better a dry crust with peace and quiet than a house full of feasting, with strife.

Proverbs 11:29
He who brings trouble on his family will inherit only wind, and the fool will be servant to the wise.

Proverbs 14:11
The house of the wicked will be destroyed, but the tent of the upright will flourish.

Proverbs 12:7
Wicked men are overthrown and are no more, but the house of the righteous stands firm.

Proverbs 15:25-27
The LORD tears down the proud man's house but he keeps the widow's boundaries intact. The LORD detests the thoughts of the wicked, but those of the pure are pleasing to him. A greedy man brings trouble to his family, but he who hates bribes will live.

Proverbs 17:13
If a man pays back evil for good, evil will never leave his house.

Psalm 78:57
Like their fathers they were disloyal and faithless, as unreliable as a faulty bow.

YOUR FAITH AFFECTS YOUR CHILDREN

Psalm 103:17
But from everlasting to everlasting the LORD's love is with those who fear him, and his righteousness with their children's children.

Proverbs 14:26
He who fears the LORD has a secure fortress, and for his children it will be a refuge.

Psalm 112:2
His children will be mighty in the land; the generation of the upright will be blessed.

Psalm 102:28
The children of your servants will live in your presence; their descendants will be established before you.

Psalm 37:25-26
I was young and now I am old, yet I have never seen the righteous forsaken or their children begging bread. They are always generous and lend freely; their children will be blessed.

Proverbs 3:33
The LORD's curse is on the house of the wicked, but he blesses the home of the righteous.

Proverbs 20:7
The righteous man leads a blameless life; blessed are his children after him.

GIVE A LEGACY THAT WILL LAST FOR GENERATIONS

Psalm 34:11
Come, my children, listen to me; I will teach you the fear of the LORD.

Psalm 145:4
One generation will commend your works to another; they will tell of your mighty acts.

Psalm 79:13
Then we your people, the sheep of your pasture, will praise you forever; from generation to generation we will recount your praise.

Psalm 102:18
Let this be written for a future generation, that a people not yet created may praise the LORD.

Psalm 71:18
Even when I am old and gray, do not forsake me, O God, till I declare your power to the next generation, your might to all who are to come.

Psalm 89:1
I will sing of the LORD's great love forever; with my mouth I will make your faithfulness known through all generations.

Psalm 44:1-3
We have heard with our ears, O God; our fathers have told us what you did in their days, in days long ago. With your hand you drove out the nations and planted our fathers; you crushed the peoples and made our fathers flourish. It was not by their sword that they won the land, nor did their arm bring them victory; it was your right hand, your arm, and the light of your face, for you loved them.

Psalm 78:4-6
We will not hide them from their children; we will tell the next generation the praiseworthy deeds of the LORD, his power, and the wonders he has done. He decreed statutes for Jacob and established the law in Israel, which he commanded our forefathers to teach their children, so the next generation would know them, even the children yet to be born, and they in turn would tell their children.

Psalm 37:18
The days of the blameless are known to the LORD, and their inheritance will endure forever.

Proverbs 13:22
A good man leaves an inheritance for his children's children, but a sinner's wealth is stored up for the righteous.

DISCIPLINE FOR THE RIGHT REASONS

Proverbs 22:6
Train a child in the way he should go, and when he is old he will not turn from it.

Proverbs 13:24
He who spares the rod hates his son, but he who loves him is careful to discipline him.

Proverbs 29:15
The rod of correction imparts wisdom, but a child left to itself disgraces his mother.

Proverbs 22:15
Folly is bound up in the heart of a child, but the rod of discipline will drive it far from him.

Proverbs 29:17
Discipline your son, and he will give you peace; he will bring delight to your soul.

Proverbs 19:18
Discipline your son, for in that there is hope; do not be a willing party to his death.

Proverbs 29:21
If a man pampers his servant from youth, he will bring grief in the end.

Proverbs 3:11-12
My son, do not despise the LORD's discipline and do not resent his rebuke, because the LORD disciplines those he loves, as a father the son he delights in.

Proverbs 23:13
Do not withhold discipline from a child; if you punish him with the rod, he will not die.

ENTRUST YOUR CHILDREN TO GOD'S CARE

Psalm 100:5
For the LORD is good and his love endures forever; his faithfulness continues through all generations.

Psalm 145:13
Your kingdom is an everlasting kingdom, and your dominion endures through all generations. The LORD is faithful to all his promises and loving toward all he has made.

Psalm 72:4
He will defend the afflicted among the people and save the children of the needy; he will crush the oppressor.

Psalm 119:89-90
Your word, O LORD, is eternal; it stands firm in the heavens. Your faithfulness continues through all generations; you established the earth, and it endures.

Psalm 135:13-14
Your name, O LORD, endures forever, your renown, O LORD, through all generations. For the LORD will vindicate his people and have compassion on his servants.

Psalm 115:14
May the LORD make you increase, both you and your children.

Psalm 90:1
LORD, you have been our dwelling place throughout all generations.

Psalm 8:2
From the lips of children and infants you have ordained praise because of your enemies, to silence the foe and the avenger.

B. Advice for Children

LISTENING TO YOUR PARENTS IS SMART

Proverbs 1:8-9
Listen, my son, to your father's instruction and do not forsake your mother's teaching. They will be a garland to grace your head and a chain to adorn your neck.

Proverbs 23:22
Listen to your father, who gave you life, and do not despise your mother when she is old.

Proverbs 4:10
Listen, my son, accept what I say, and the years of your life will be many.

Proverbs 13:1
A wise son heeds his father's instruction, but a mocker does not listen to rebuke.

Proverbs 15:5
A fool spurns his father's discipline, but whoever heeds correction shows prudence.

Proverbs 19:20
Listen to advice and accept instruction, and in the end you will be wise.

Proverbs 10:8
The wise in heart accept commands, but a chattering fool comes to ruin.

Proverbs 15:31
He who listens to a life-giving rebuke will be at home among the wise.

Proverbs 9:8-9
Do not rebuke a mocker or he will hate you; rebuke a wise man and he will love you. Instruct a wise man and he will

be wiser still; teach a righteous man and he will add to his learning.

Proverbs 15:12
A mocker resents correction; he will not consult the wise.

Proverbs 12:15
The way of a fool seems right to him, but a wise man listens to advice.

Proverbs 25:12
Like an earring of gold or an ornament of fine gold is a wise man's rebuke to a listening ear.

Proverbs 21:11
When a mocker is punished, the simple gain wisdom; when a wise man is instructed, he gets knowledge.

Proverbs 30:17
The eye that mocks a father, that scorns obedience to a mother, will be pecked out by the ravens of the valley, will be eaten by the vultures.

Proverbs 28:24
He who robs his father or mother and says, "It's not wrong"—he is partner to him who destroys.

Proverbs 19:27
Stop listening to instruction, my son, and you will stray from the words of knowledge.

CHOOSE YOUR FRIENDS WISELY

Proverbs 13:20
He who walks with the wise grows wise, but a companion of fools suffers harm.

Proverbs 27:6
The kisses of an enemy may be profuse, but faithful are the wounds of a friend.

Proverbs 17:17
A friend loves at all times, and a brother is born for adversity.

Proverbs 27:9
Perfume and incense bring joy to the heart, and the pleasantness of one's friend springs from his earnest counsel.

Proverbs 28:7
He who keeps the law is a discerning son, but a companion of gluttons disgraces his father.

Proverbs 17:9
He who covers over an offense promotes love, but whoever repeats the matter separates close friends.

Proverbs 22:24
Do not make friends with a hot-tempered man, do not associate with one easily angered.

Proverbs 24:21-22
Fear the LORD and the king, my son, and do not join with the rebellious, for those two will send sudden destruction upon them, and who knows what calamities they can bring?

Proverbs 29:3
A man who loves wisdom brings joy to his father, but a companion of prostitutes squanders his wealth.

Proverbs 16:28
A perverse man stirs up dissension, and a gossip separates close friends.

Proverbs 1:10
My son, if sinners entice you, do not give in to them.

Proverbs 18:24
A man of many companions may come to ruin, but there is a friend who sticks closer than a brother.

YOUR BEHAVIOR AFFECTS YOUR FAMILY

Proverbs 15:20
A wise son brings joy to his father, but a foolish man despises his mother.

Proverbs 23:15
My son, if your heart is wise, then my heart will be glad.

Proverbs 23:22-25
Listen to your father, who gave you life, and do not despise your mother when she is old. Buy the truth and do not sell it; get wisdom, discipline and understanding. The father of a righteous man has great joy; he who has a wise son delights in him. May your father and mother be glad; may she who gave you birth rejoice!

Proverbs 10:1
A wise son brings joy to his father, but a foolish son grief to his mother.

Proverbs 20:20
If a man curses his father or mother, his lamp will be snuffed out in pitch darkness.

Proverbs 17:21
To have a fool for a son brings grief; there is no joy for the father of a fool.

Proverbs 27:11
Be wise, my son, and bring joy to my heart; then I can answer anyone who treats me with contempt.

Proverbs 19:26
He who robs his father and drives out his mother is a son who brings shame and disgrace.

Proverbs 29:3
A man who loves wisdom brings joy to his father, but a companion of prostitutes squanders his wealth.

Proverbs 17:25
A foolish son brings grief to his father and bitterness to the one who bore him.

Proverbs 19:13
A foolish son is his father's ruin, and a quarrelsome wife is like a constant dripping.

Psalm 133:1
How good and pleasant it is when brothers live together in unity!

Proverbs 18:19
An offended brother is more unyielding than a fortified city, and disputes are like the barred gates of a citadel.

RIGHT ATTITUDES PRODUCE RIGHT ACTIONS

Proverbs 23:19
Listen, my son, and be wise, and keep your heart on the right path.

Proverbs 20:11
Even a child is known by his actions, by whether his conduct is pure and right.

Proverbs 14:16
A wise man fears the LORD and shuns evil, but a fool is
hotheaded and reckless.

Proverbs 3:35
The wise inherit honor, but fools he holds up to shame.

Proverbs 16:21-23
The wise in heart are called discerning, and pleasant
words promote instruction. Understanding is a fountain
of life to those who have it, but folly brings punishment
to fools. A wise man's heart guides his mouth, and his lips
promote instruction.

Proverbs 20:1
Wine is a mocker and beer a brawler; whoever is led astray
by them is not wise.

Proverbs 10:5
He who gathers crops in summer is a wise son, but he who
sleeps during harvest is a disgraceful son.

Proverbs 10:19
When words are many, sin is not absent, but he who holds
his tongue is wise.

Proverbs 17:2
A wise servant will rule over a disgraceful son, and will
share the inheritance as one of the brothers.

Proverbs 3:5-7
Trust in the LORD with all your heart and lean not on your own understanding; in all your ways acknowledge him, and he will make your paths straight. Do not be wise in your own eyes; fear the LORD and shun evil.

Proverbs 10:14
Wise men store up knowledge, but the mouth of a fool invites ruin.

Psalm 27:10
Though my father and mother forsake me, the LORD will receive me.

ADDITIONAL
31-DAY
EXPERIMENTS

Now that you have finished a month of studying God's Word and building a strong family, I hope you will want to continue to spend time alone with our wonderful Lord each day. He is the Vine from whom you can receive life and nourishment. Intimacy with Him continues and increases as you daily walk with Him.

The *31-Day Experiment* series of books has been designed to help you develop a consistent devotional time with your heavenly Father. Whether you are a new Christian or have been one for a long time, these books will help you experience for yourself the joy of discovering God's truth from the Bible.

Although all the books are designed like the one you have just completed, each one focuses on different themes and passages for you to study.

At the end of each Experiment is a number of simple Bible study methods or ideas for further growth. These will help you investigate, on your own, more of the truth that the Holy Spirit has given for you to know in the Bible.

These books are designed to help you get into God's Word, and get God's Word into you:

1. GROWING CLOSER TO GOD

Do you want a deeper oneness with the Lord? This book is designed to cultivate your relationship with God by looking at passages that will help you discover truths that are foundational to knowing the Lord intimately. You'll learn about His purpose and plan for you, and about how to be transformed from the inside out.

2. A PERSONAL EXPERIMENT IN FAITH-BUILDING

Begin to see your confidence in God develop into a more consistent trust. Your faith will grow as you learn to apply God's Word to your life and expect Christ to accomplish great things through you. You will never be the same as you discover how Christ built the faith of His disciples—and how He can do the same for you.

3. STANDING STRONG IN A GODLESS CULTURE

Try this Experiment and find out what it takes to walk powerfully with God and hold onto biblical values regardless of society's pressures. It will help you develop strength for your personal needs, wisdom to make tough choices, and courage to face complex problems.

4. KNOWING GOD'S HEART, SHARING HIS JOY

Find your special place in God's heart and eternal plan. Gain a clearer insight into God's life-changing message for all people. As a result, you will learn to become a more effective witness for Christ. By understanding God's heart, you'll be freed to share the plan of salvation with others—naturally and enthusiastically.

5. BUILDING A POSITIVE SELF-IMAGE

Would you like to have greater confidence to become all that God wants you to be? This book will help you develop a healthy biblical perspective about yourself as you look into God's Word. He will strengthen your self-image as you focus on what God has created you to be. You will discover new self-confidence, joy, and direction for your life.

6. KNOWING GOD BY HIS NAMES

Spend one month discovering how God has revealed Himself through His many names. You will study 31 of God's names that give you significant insights into His character and how He meets your needs. Learn how the Heavenly Father provides for you, the Prince of Peace calms your anxieties, and the Shepherd guides you. As you meditate on God's character, you will get to know Him better and enjoy a more intimate relationship with Him.

7. MAKING A GOOD MARRIAGE EVEN BETTER

Have you ever wondered what the Bible says about developing a marriage that will last a lifetime? As you work through this Experiment book you will learn about God's instructions for a top-quality husband-wife relationship. There are no personal opinions given by me or any other human author. It will be just you, God, and the Scriptures interacting together to make your marriage better than ever.

ABOUT THE AUTHOR

Dick Purnell is a man who loves his wife, his kids and helping other couples build strong families.

He and Paula speak together at FamilyLife Marriage Conferences throughout the country. Dick has served as a pastor in Indiana and is now the founder and director of Single Life Resources, a ministry of Campus Crusade for Christ. During his 32 years of ministry he has endeavored to help people base their lives on biblical truths.

A graduate of Wheaton College, Dick holds a Master of Divinity degree from Trinity Evangelical Divinity School and a master's degree in education (specializing in counseling) from Indiana University.

Dick is the author of *Becoming a Friend and Lover, Free to Love Again: Coming to Terms with Sexual Regret* and *Building a Relationship That Lasts.* He has also written eight books in the *31-Day Experiment* Bible study series.

Dick and Paula have two daughters, Rachel and Ashley. They love living in North Carolina.